A New Geyser Erupts

Written by Matilda May

Illustrated by Wesley Lowe

Flying Start
to Literacy®

Contents

Chapter 1

Whoosh!   4

Chapter 2

Screams in the dark   10

Chapter 3

Stranded   18

Chapter 4

Geyser erupting   26

Whoosh!

It was early in the morning when Ranger Kate suddenly sat up in bed. What was that strange noise? It sounded like a train.

"What? It can't be a train," Kate said. "But what is it?"

She jumped out of bed and ran outside. Through the trees she could see steam rising into the air.

Whoosh!

"It's the Cloud Buster Geyser. I have to go and see it!"

This was Peach Sands National Park's tallest geyser and no one had seen it erupt for years. The national park included a huge volcanic area that had hundreds of geysers and bubbling mud pools.

Kate dressed quickly, then grabbed her walkie-talkie and attached it to her belt. Just as she was about to leave the cabin, she turned back and grabbed her flare gun, some flares and a torch. She was trying to remember her training – be prepared for any emergency. She switched on the torch. Good – it was working.

Kate jumped into her truck and drove to the Peach Sands' car park. She then walked carefully along the path that led to the geyser.

The whooshing and roaring got louder.

"Woo-hoo!" yelled Kate over the noise.

As Kate stood and watched the geyser blow its load of boiling water and steam high into the air, she called the rangers' station on her walkie-talkie.

"Ranger Kate to Base," Kate called into her walkie-talkie.

"Go ahead," said Ranger Lupe.

"I'm at the Cloud Buster Geyser and it's erupting!" Kate shouted excitedly.

"Wow! Is that what that noise was?" said Lupe. "That's the first time in years. You're very lucky to see it."

"Yeah, I know. It's amazing! You should see it, Lupe! It's so high, it's . . ."

"Kate, while you're there I need you to do something important," interrupted Lupe. "Kate, can you hear me?"

But Kate was busy patting her pockets, looking for her phone. She wanted to take a photo of the geyser with its jet of boiling water shooting up high into the sky.

"Kate, are you listening?" Lupe sounded annoyed.

Kate quickly paid attention.

"Yes, Lupe, of course."

"Some of the boardwalks towards the hill trail are due for repair, so they have been closed off. Can you make sure the barriers and warning signs are still up so no one goes on them?" asked Lupe.

"Yeah, sure," said Kate, still watching the geyser. She hoped it wouldn't stop before she had a chance to take that photo, but she'd checked all her pockets – no phone!

"And Kate, please be careful. I don't want to remind you about what happened last month."

Kate felt a wave of shame and fear.

"I'll be careful," she said quietly. Then she added firmly, "You can count on me, Lupe. I'll radio in and give you updates. Over and out."

Kate squeezed her eyes shut to block out the images that came into her head from that dreadful night a month ago, but it was too late.

Chapter 2

Screams in the dark

Kate would never forget that terrible night.

Her best friend Dayna was visiting. Kate and Dayna had been the stars of their high school gymnastics team. But when Kate injured her back, she had to give it up. Dayna was about to compete in a major gymnastics competition, but had taken time out to visit her friend in her new job.

The trip had been planned for months. Kate was excited about spending time with her friend.

Each day, they went on hikes and had picnics. Kate showed Dayna all her favourite places in the park – the geysers, the bubbling mud pools and the turquoise blue ponds of boiling water.

On Dayna's last evening, they walked through the hills to watch the sunset. Kate took a torch and her walkie-talkie and they headed off.

The sunset was beautiful. They stayed and watched as the dusk turned to twilight and the stars came out. The bubbling and gurgling noises of the nearby thermal pools seemed louder in the still air.

"Okay, we'd better get back while we can still see," said Kate.

"I wish I didn't have to leave," said Dayna, "but I've got to get up early for the bus back to the city."

The friends started to make their way down the hill. The air was getting colder, and Kate wished they had brought warmer jackets. The shapes of the rocks and hollows were now just all shadows and difficult to tell apart.

"Ow!" said Kate, as she banged her shin on a rock. "Time to use the torch."

She unhooked it from her belt and clicked it on. It flickered weakly, then went out.

"Oh, no!" said Dayna, as she took the torch from Kate. She shook it and clicked it off and on. Nothing. "But you know your way in the dark, don't you?"

"Yeah, sure. Just follow me and walk in my steps, so you don't step in a hole."

"That would be a disaster," said Dayna. "I need to be in good shape for the gymnastics competition next week."

Kate was annoyed with herself and a bit worried, but she couldn't let Dayna see it. Maybe she should call Lupe? Kate reached for her walkie-talkie then stopped. Lupe would not be impressed with the fact that Kate had not checked her torch before she left. This was the first thing they were told to do before setting out each day – check your equipment.

She breathed in deeply and stepped carefully down the hill, peering into the gloom. Her eyes adjusted slightly and she began to feel more confident.

"Look, we can see the light from my cabin. We're nearly there." Kate was relieved. Even though she couldn't find the path, the lights from her cabin would guide her.

"Good," said Dayna. She rubbed her arms. "It's freezing. I hope I don't get a cramp." She stretched her legs. "Come on, let's hurry." Dayna pushed ahead of Kate and began to walk quickly.

"Wait, Dayna. You don't know where to go. You have to follow me."

But Dayna had disappeared. Then, suddenly, there was a gasp and a scream.

"Kate, Kate!" Then scream after scream.

Kate made her way quickly down the slope in the direction of Dayna's scream. Her friend was huddled on the ground, clutching her foot. She was sobbing and screaming.

Kate leaned down.

"What? Have you twisted your ankle?"

Then she saw Dayna's foot, covered in mud. Her foot
had broken through a crust of ground and into boiling
mud. Kate ripped at the shoelaces on Dayna's shoe. She
ignored the pain in her hands as she quickly pulled off
the hot, muddy shoe. Dayna was screaming and crying.
In the dim light, her foot looked red and white. It was
badly burnt and swelling quickly.

Kate pulled her walkie-talkie off her belt.

"Ranger Kate to Base! Ranger Kate to Base! Please come in, Lupe!" She barely waited before she tried again. "Lupe, please! I need your help!" She gasped and felt dizzy. It didn't seem real, like she was in a terrible dream.

"I'm here Kate, what is it? Is everything okay?"

"Lupe, this is an emergency!" Kate explained the situation quickly. Lupe was calm and commanding. She called in the other rangers. They managed to find them in the dark, after lots of shouting. They carried Dayna out to the ambulance that drove the hour into town to the hospital.

The next day, Kate was reprimanded severely. Lupe could not believe that Kate hadn't checked her torch.

"You didn't check your torch, and where was your flare, Kate? Why didn't you have one with you?"

"I didn't think . . ." stammered Kate, embarrassed. "I didn't think I would need one."

"It would have helped the rangers to find your position."

"I'm sorry, Lupe."

"It's a dangerous job being a ranger," explained Lupe. "We have to make sure that you know what to do in an emergency. And you must be prepared for an emergency at all times."

Kate got an official warning. And cadets only got one warning. Another incident and that would be the end of Kate's park ranger career.

Chapter 3

Stranded

Suddenly, Kate snapped back to reality. The boardwalk was vibrating. Earthquake! She crouched down for safety and waited for it to pass. This was one of the most dangerous areas of the park. All around her, hot springs and mud pools boiled and bubbled.

There were many more steam clouds than usual, hissing up from the fissures in the ground, like dozens of boiling kettles. There was no wind and the whole area was covered in steam.

"Base to Ranger Kate! Base to Ranger Kate!" crackled Kate's walkie-talkie. "Are you okay, Kate? That was a huge tremor," said Lupe.

"I'm okay, Lupe. I'm almost at the warning sign, but there's a lot of steam, so I'm going to have to walk further."

"Come back, Kate. I don't want you out there in case there's another tremor. Those boardwalks are old and they might be unsafe," said Lupe.

Up ahead, Kate could see a bright orange mesh fence and a warning sign across the boardwalk.

"It's okay. I can see the sign and the barrier. It's still up," said Kate. "Oh, but wait, what about the barrier at the other end of the boardwalk, Lupe? Don't I need to check that?"

"Don't worry, Kate. Just come back to Base."

Lupe sounded concerned.

But Kate was already stepping over the orange mesh barrier. Some boards were missing, but Kate stepped over the gaps and kept walking. The boardwalk felt slightly wobbly. Should she keep going?

"I'm nearly there. I should be nearly at the . . ." Kate gasped. Another tremor! The boardwalk wobbled and Kate almost fell. To keep her balance, she flung her arms up in the air. The walkie-talkie flew out of her hand and into the boiling water.

That's when she heard a voice calling through the steam, as she crouched down again and gripped the boards.

It was a child's voice. Kate peered through the steam, but she couldn't see anyone.

"Help!" cried the voice again.

Kate looked behind her. She should go back. She didn't know what lay ahead, and she had no walkie-talkie to call for back up if anyone needed rescuing. Lupe always said, "Don't go into danger alone!"

But she knew she had to go and help. She turned back to the voice.

"I'm coming, just wait right there," yelled Kate.

"Please hurry!" called another voice. Kate began to walk quickly but carefully on the boardwalk, testing each plank before putting her weight on it.

Then there was a breeze and the steam cleared. Kate could see a family of hikers huddled on the boardwalk.

As Kate approached the family, she saw that the boardwalk between her and the hikers had tipped slightly . . . and some of the boards had broken up.

The family was terrified.

"We can't go back the way we came. I was last and when I stepped on the boardwalk, some of the boards broke. I nearly fell," shouted the woman fearfully, hugging her children to her.

Kate looked past them to where they had walked. The boardwalk leading towards the hot springs and mud pools had a large gap. It was too large for most people to jump across.

Kate hesitated. Could she get them to safety by herself?

"Can't we just get off and walk on the ground on this side? It looks solid," said the woman as she moved over to look at the ground.

"No!" shouted Kate and flung out her hands. She remembered what had happened to Dayna. "Stop! It's not safe. There could be boiling mud under that dirt. Do not move!"

The children were shocked at Kate's shouting and the little girl began to cry.

"Mummy, I want to go back."

"It's okay, I can help you. I'll come to you and help you across this way," said Kate. She stepped carefully on the remaining beam of the boardwalk, thanking her gymnastics training for her balance.

"No way. That's too narrow to walk along. I have terrible balance," said the woman.

"Don't you have a walkie-talkie?" asked the boy, looking at Kate's belt.

"I lost it," said Kate, and she saw their faces drop in disappointment.

Then she remembered her flare gun. Quickly, she unclipped it from the holster and loaded it with a flare.

"Okay everyone, block your ears."

The flare rocketed high into the air and exploded with a loud bang, releasing a plume of orange smoke.

"They'll see that at the Base. It's an emergency flare so back up should be here soon," said Kate. "This section of boardwalk that we're on is safe so it's best if we just wait here."

Kate turned to the children. "This is exciting. You have experienced a real earthquake. That's something you can tell your friends at school."

Kate tried to sound cheerful, but she was scared. It would take Lupe at least 20 minutes to get to them. She hoped there was not going to be another earthquake.

Chapter 4

Geyser erupting

"Wait, what's that sound?" asked the woman, looking at the ground.

There was a gentle hissing, and a column of steam rose up into the air, right next to where they were huddled on the boardwalk.

Then there was a splutter. Water splattered the boardwalk and more steam shot up.

"What's happening?" screamed the girl, as more boiling water spluttered up higher.

Kate and the woman shielded the children with their arms.

"I think it's a new geyser!" said Kate. "I'm going to have to get you all out of here right now!"

She looked around for something to help her. Then, down the end of the boardwalk on the ground, she saw a bright shape. She squinted. It was a large piece of plastic and under it was a pile of timber to repair the boardwalk.

She looked down at the boardwalk leading to the edge of the thermal basin. It was in bad shape. She looked at the gap. She hesitated. She would have to jump it. She judged it carefully, then leapt over and landed, crouching so she didn't lose her balance.

"Please hurry!" yelled the woman. More boiling water spluttered up.

Kate ran until she reached the timber. A long, wide plank jutted out. Perfect! She dragged it out and along the ground. Splinters pricked her hands. She walked quickly, panting. Steam swirled around the family as the geyser gathered its strength, ready to blow.

Kate pushed the plank across the gap.

"Quick, drag it across!" she yelled. The woman pulled the plank towards them until it reached across the gap.

Kate shuffled along towards them. "I'll help you across."

The little girl went first. She held her mother's hand and reached out her hand to Kate, who said, "Look at me, don't look down and just shuffle across."

The girl did what she was told and soon they both reached the other side.

"Now go quickly to the end and hide behind the pile of timber."

The boy did the same, and then finally the mother.
Just as she was safely across, steam and boiling water
exploded into the air.

Kate and the woman ran to safety. From behind the pile
of timber, they watched the newest geyser at Peach Sands.

Above the roar of the geyser, Kate heard a shout. It was Lupe!

"What's happened, Kate? I saw the flare. Is everything okay?"

Kate nodded. "I'm okay now, but look!" She pointed at the geyser. Lupe shielded her eyes and watched it for a moment.

"Well, what do you know? Another one! But Kate, I've been trying to reach you. Where is your walkie-talkie?" Then Lupe saw the family, who were now calm.

"I had to rescue this family, Lupe. The boardwalk was broken and we were stranded, right next to the geyser," Kate began to explain.

"What? You went on the boardwalk? Didn't you guys see the warning?"

They all turned to look as Lupe pointed. But the warning sign had fallen and was partly hidden in tall grass. The orange mesh barrier lay on the ground in a roll. No one had put it up.

"I'm sorry," said Lupe. "You were very lucky."

"I'll say we were lucky," said the woman. "Lucky that Kate came when she did. She did a fantastic rescue job. I don't like to think about what would have happened if she hadn't come along."

"She helped me walk on the plank," said the little girl, and she clasped Kate's hand. "I didn't look down."

"Wow, did she? Aren't you brave?" said Lupe. "You sure were lucky that Ranger Kate was there to help you." She looked up at Kate. "We'll have to file a report on this, Kate. Then we have some things to discuss."

Kate bit her lip. Was this it? Would Lupe fire her because she had dropped her walkie-talkie? And she hadn't returned to Base when she was told to? Tears pricked her eyes. She said goodbye to the family, then she and Lupe put up the barrier and the warning sign.

Three weeks later, Kate stood on the boardwalk in front of the column of steam rising from the new geyser.

"And here, ladies and gentlemen, boys and girls, is our newest geyser. It is only three weeks old and I was standing right here when it first erupted," said Kate.

Suddenly, there was a loud *whoosh*! A column of boiling water shot high into the sky.

"And today the new geyser is erupting just for you! It's just another day at one of the world's biggest volcanoes!" said Kate, Peach Sands' newest park ranger.